CUNT FACE SERIES

Amusing Swear Words To Color

For Stress Releasing

By
Queenie McJody

Happy Coloring!

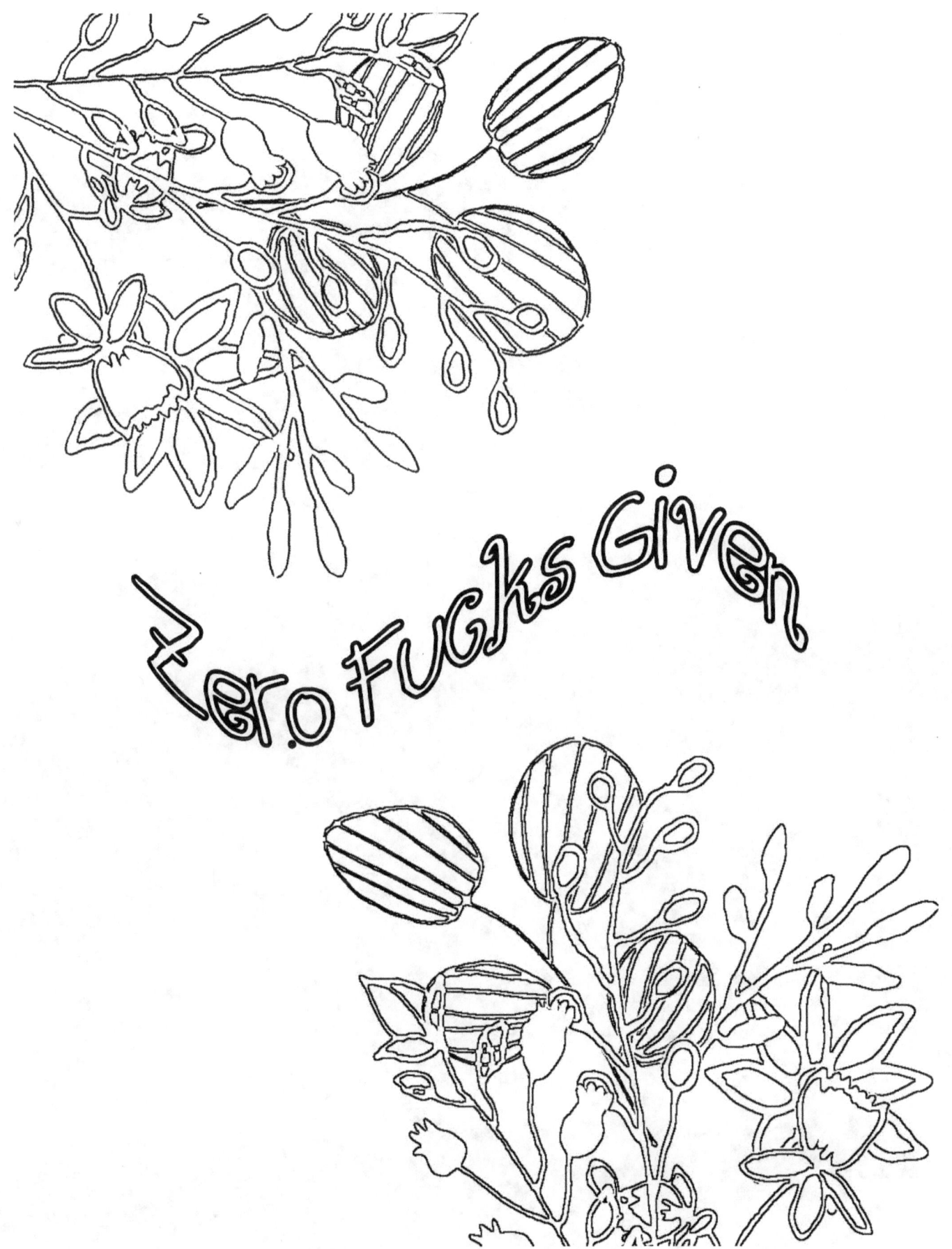

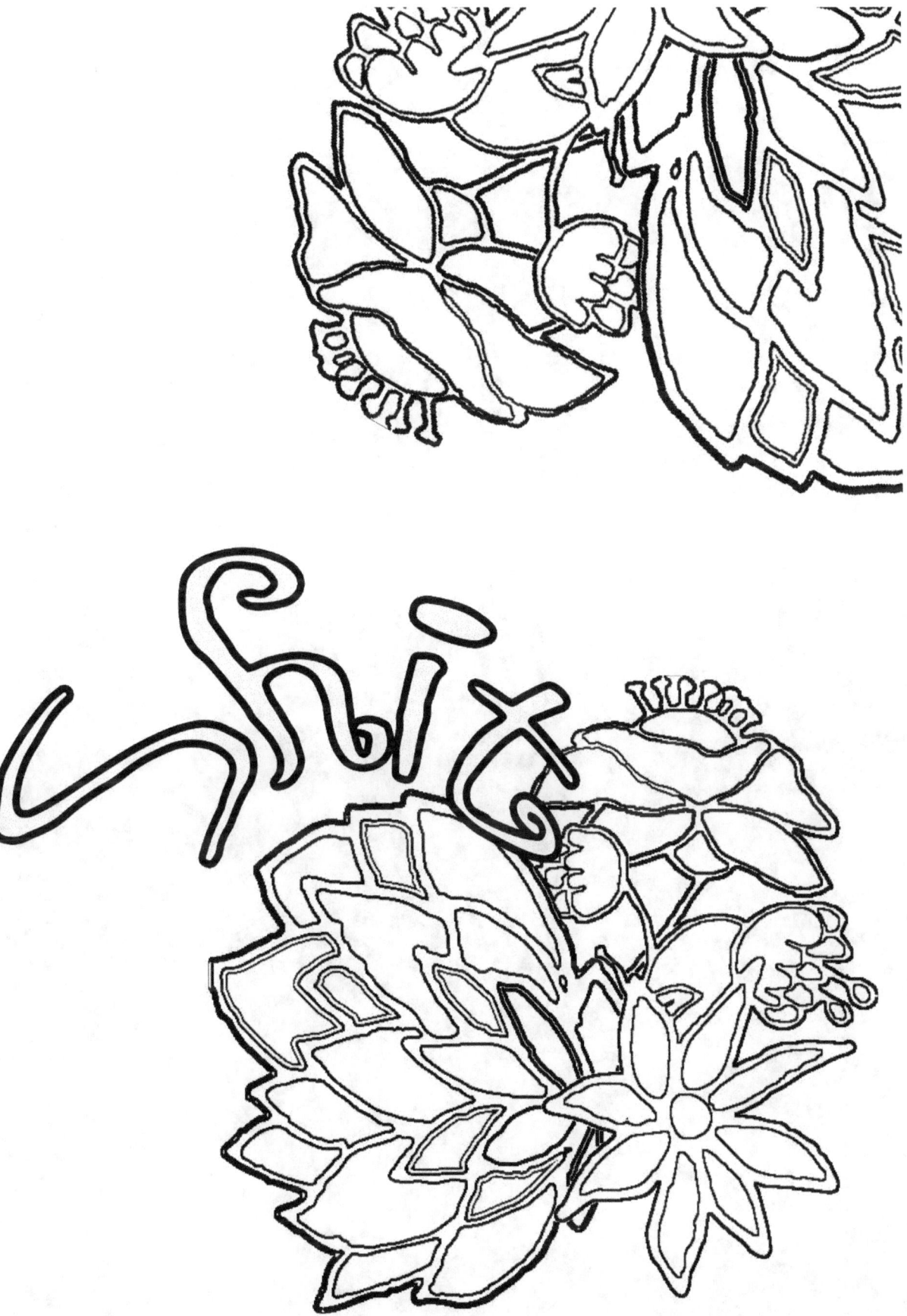

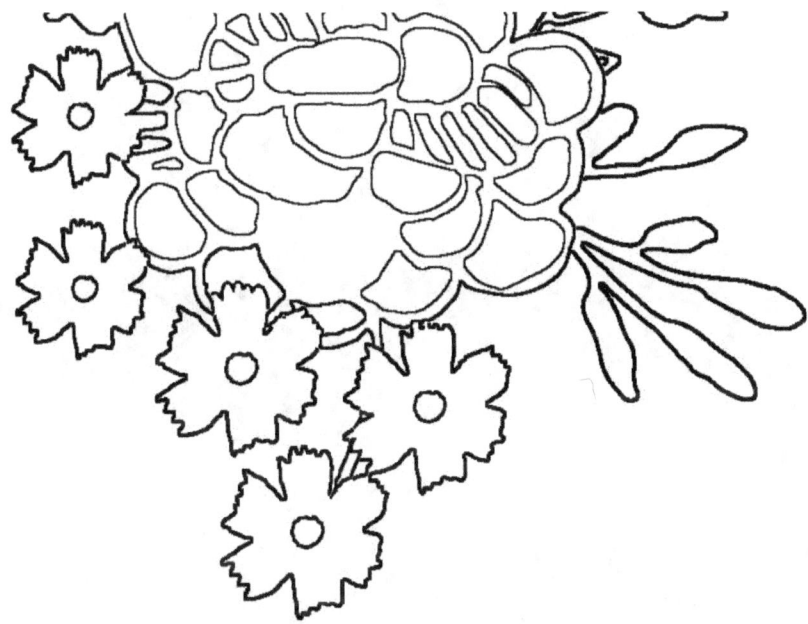

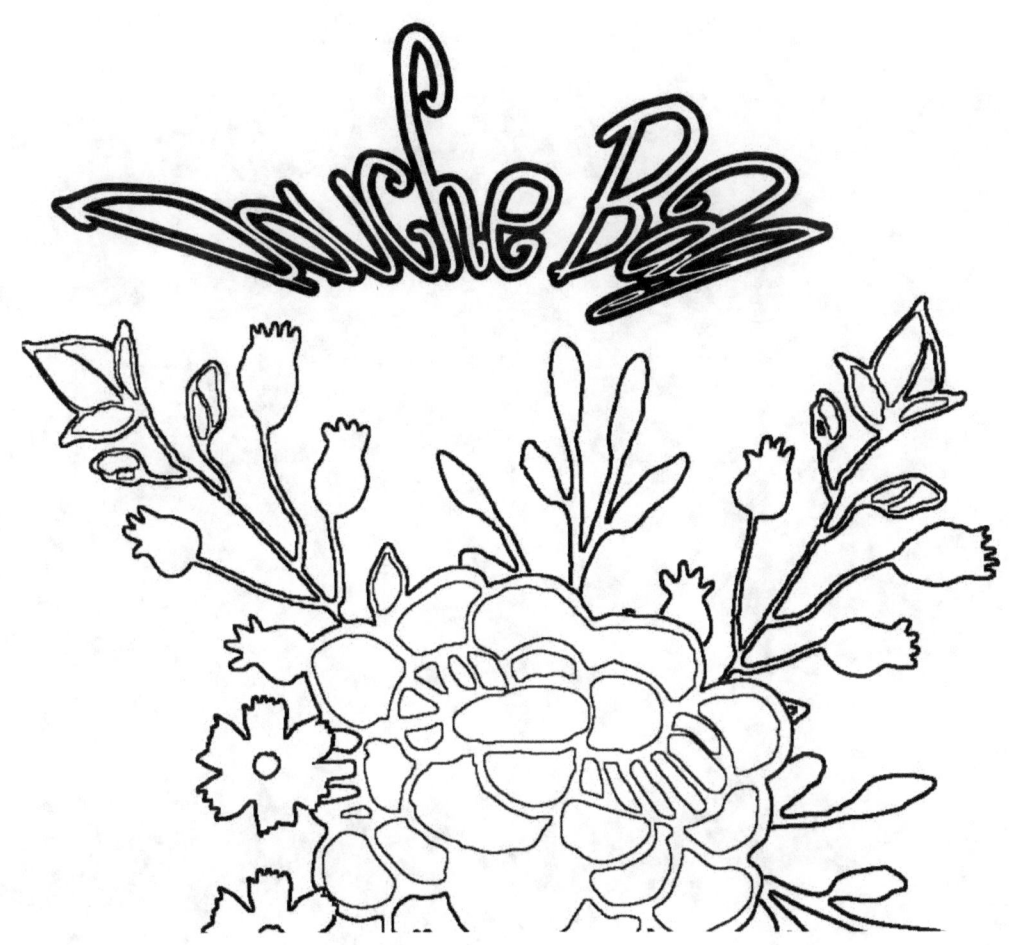

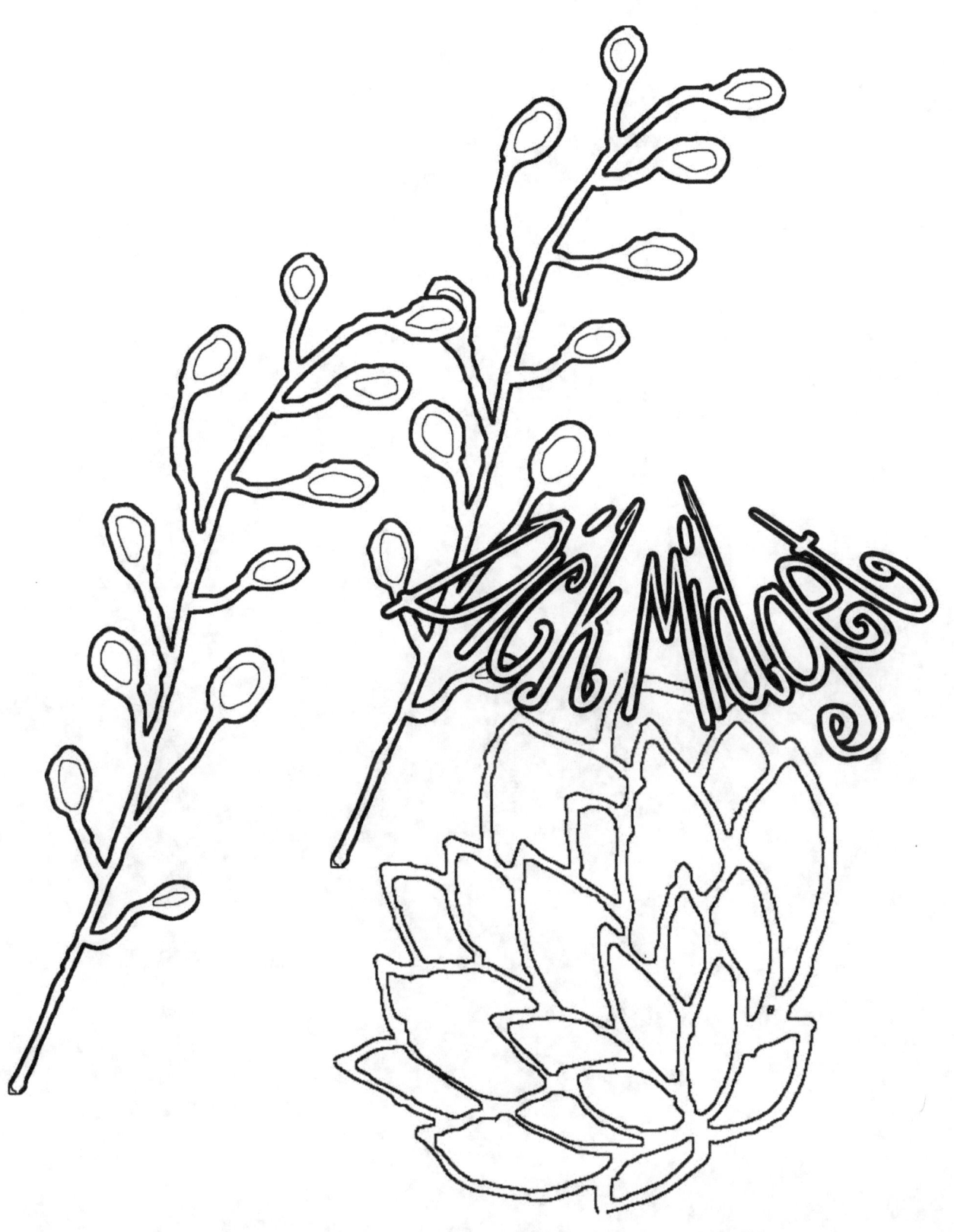

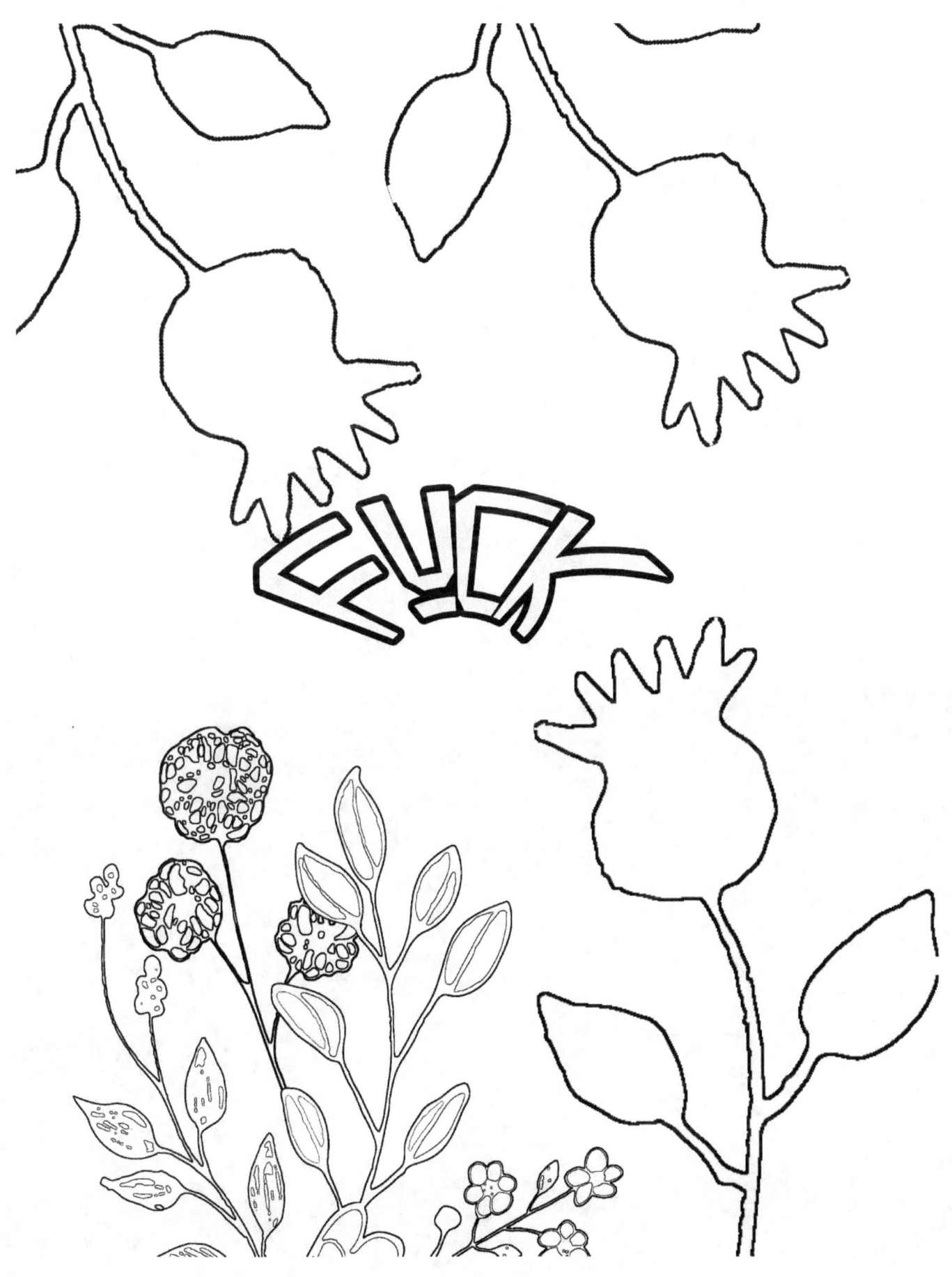

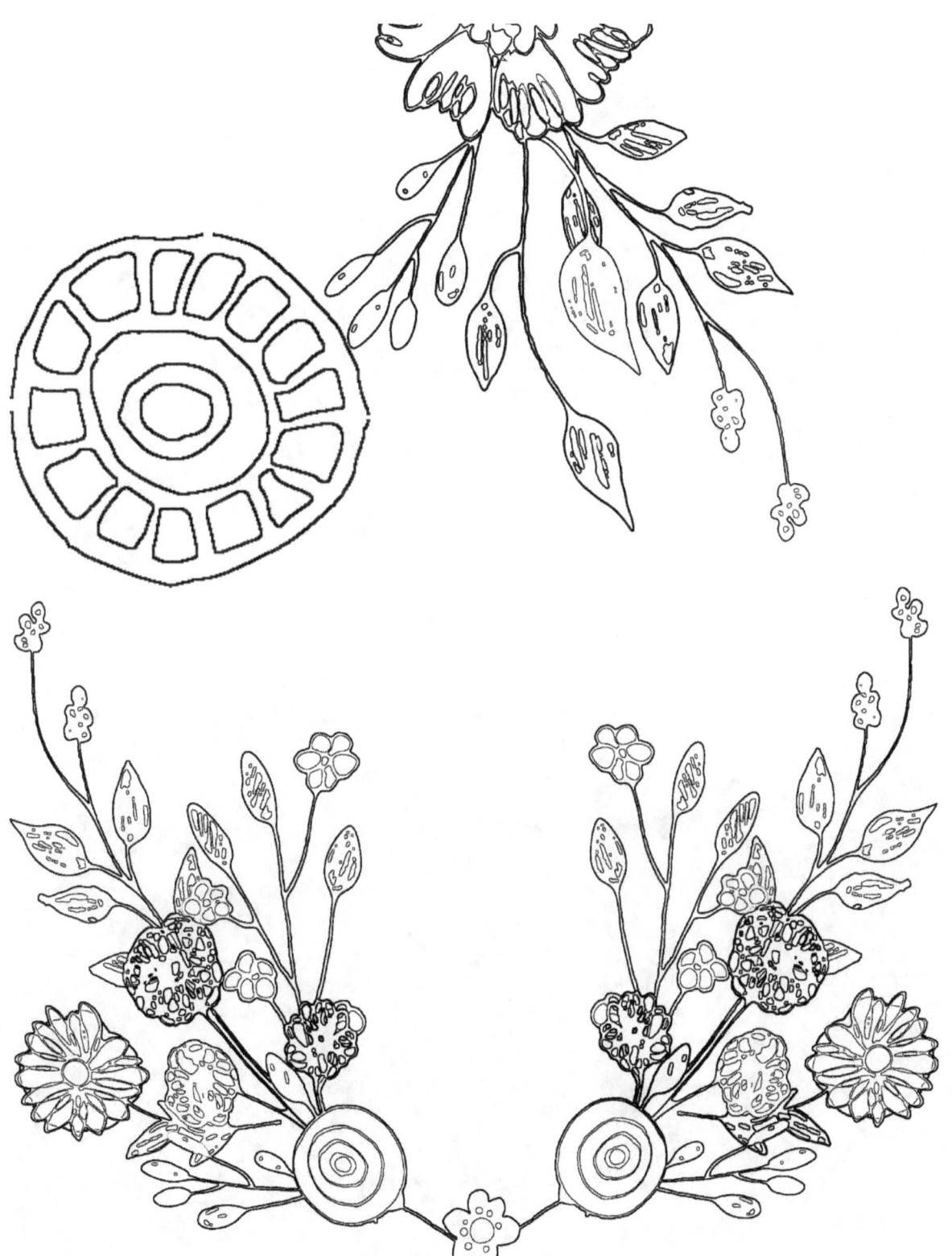

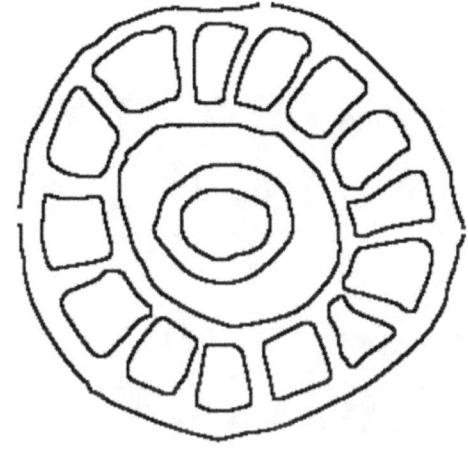

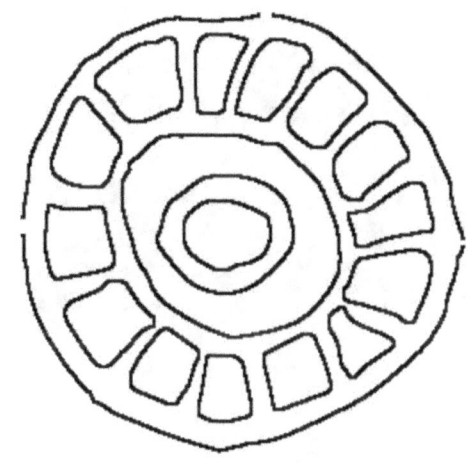

HOLLYFUCK

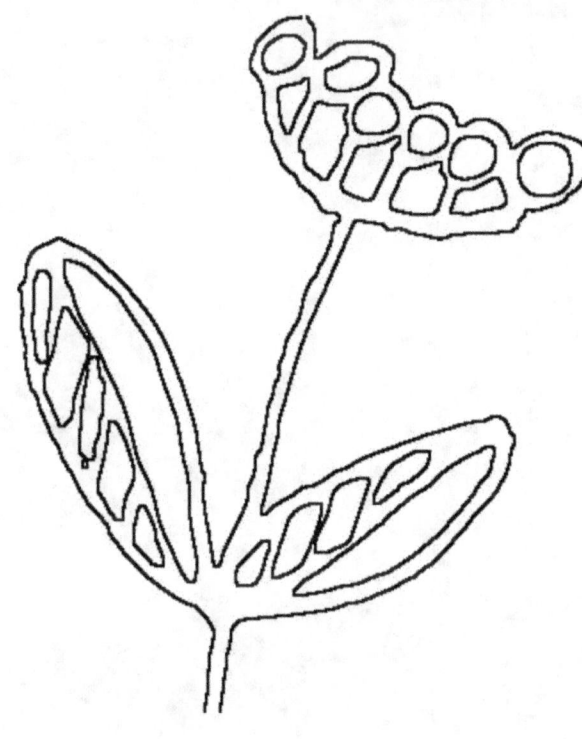

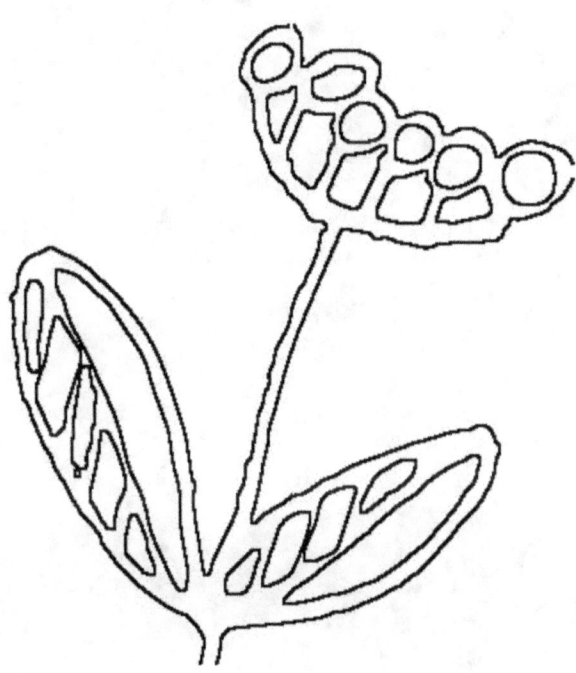

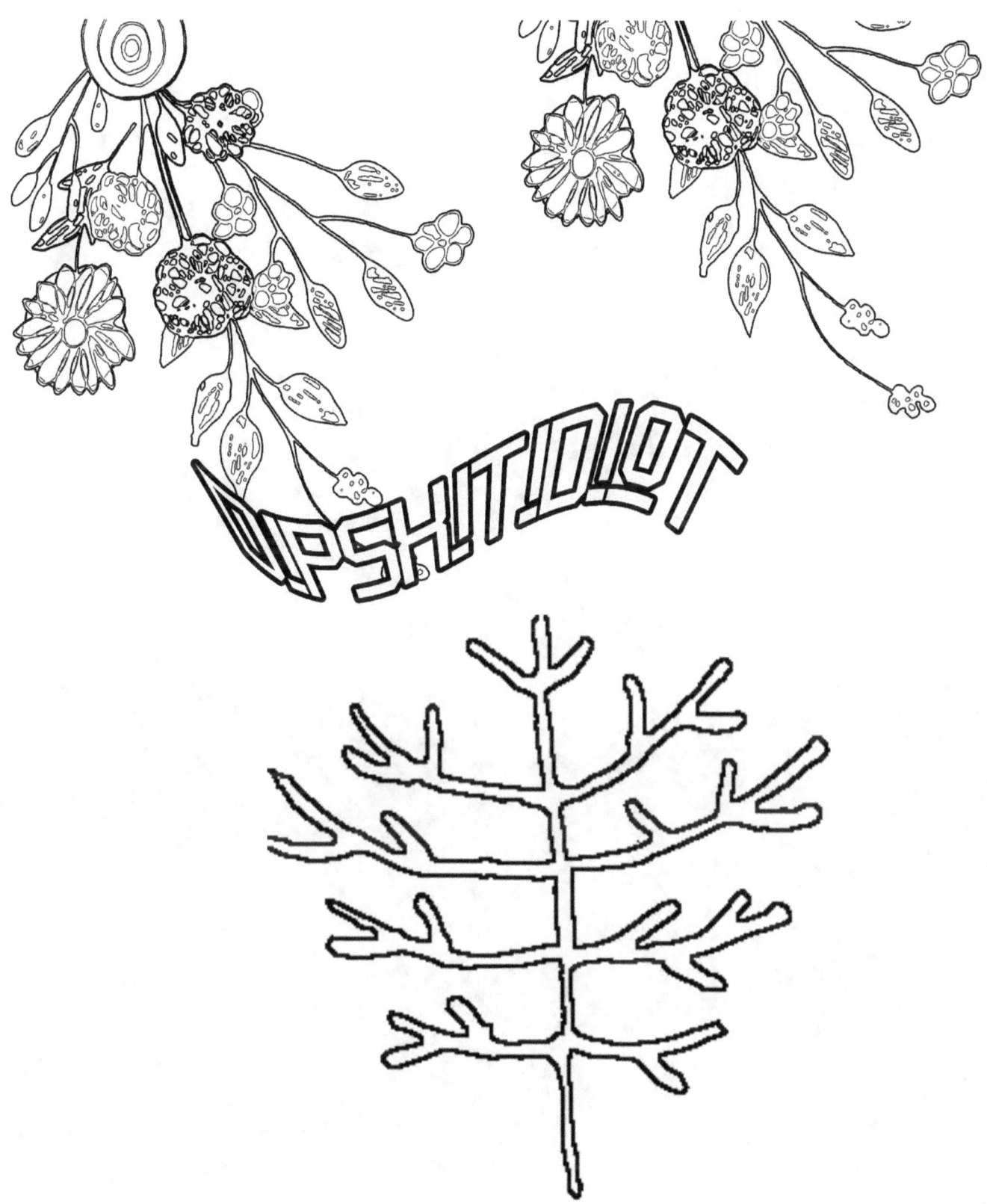

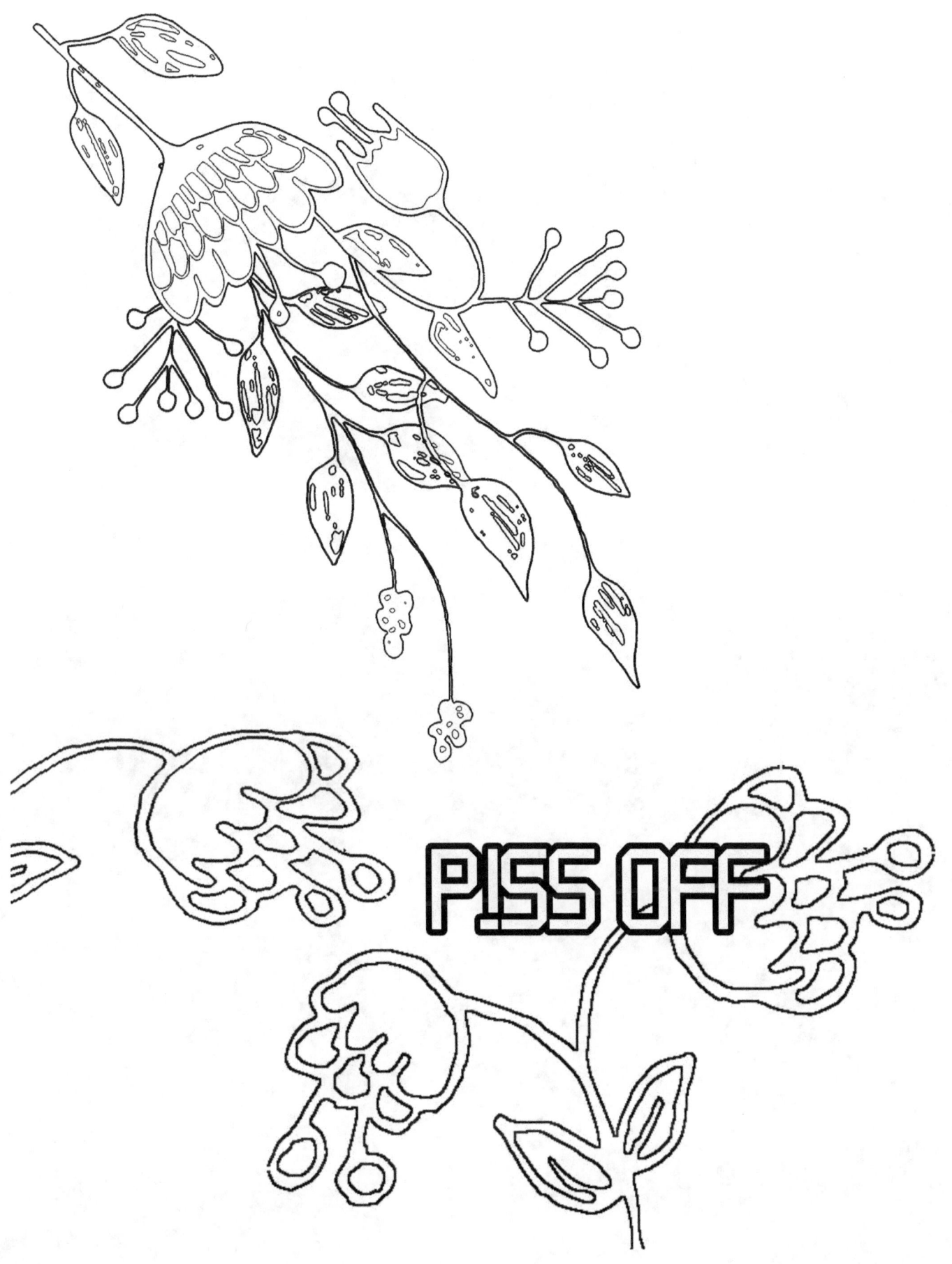

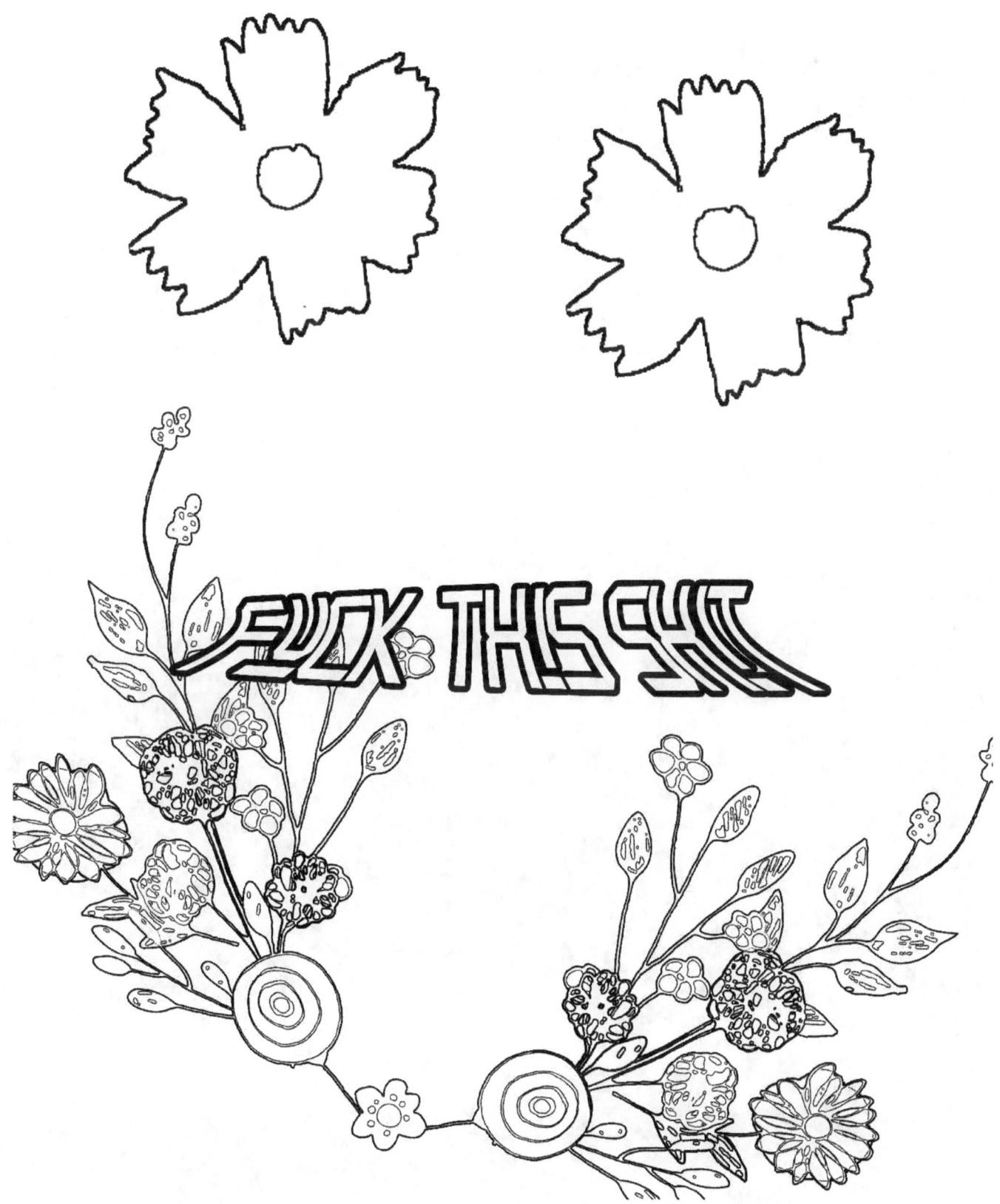

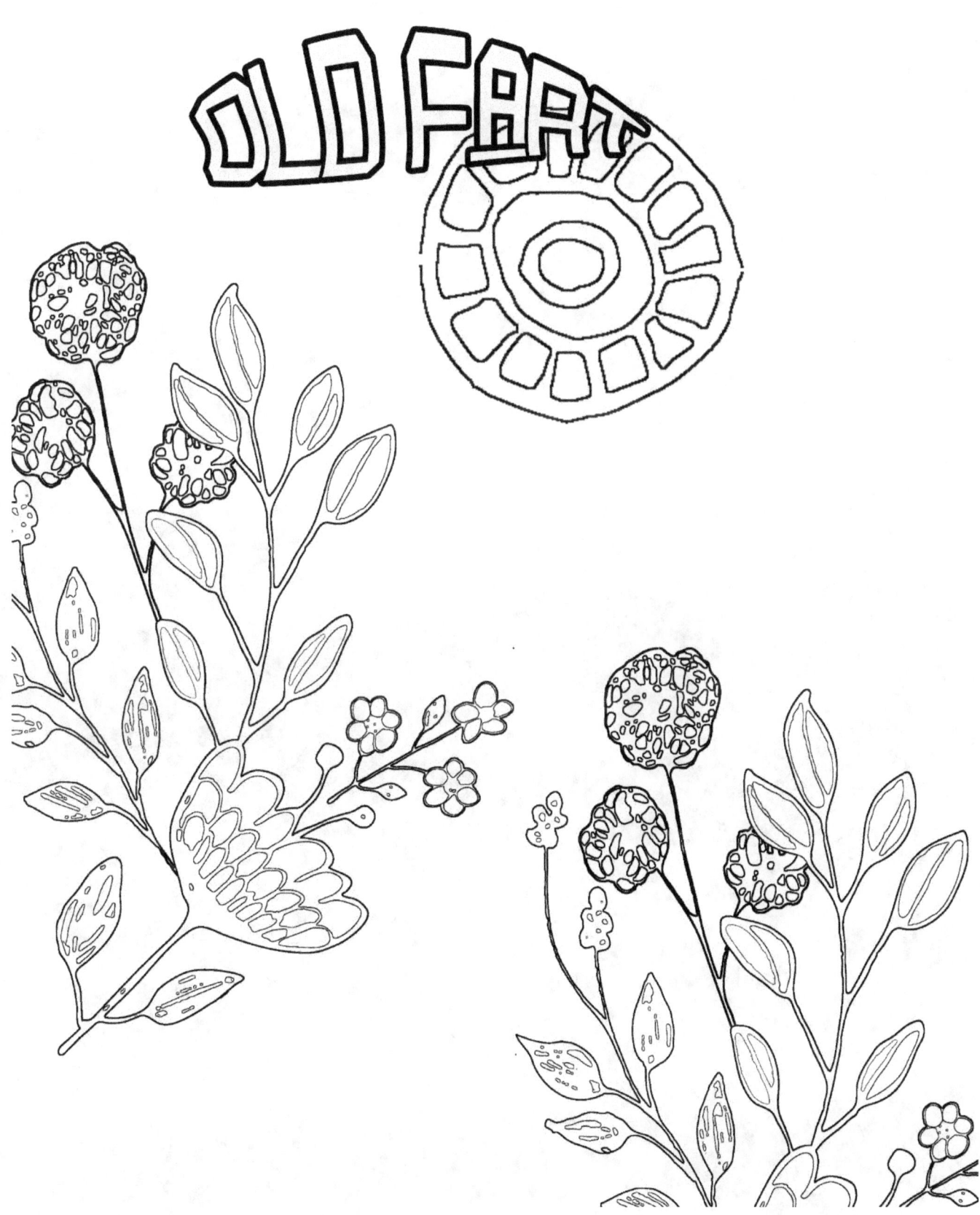

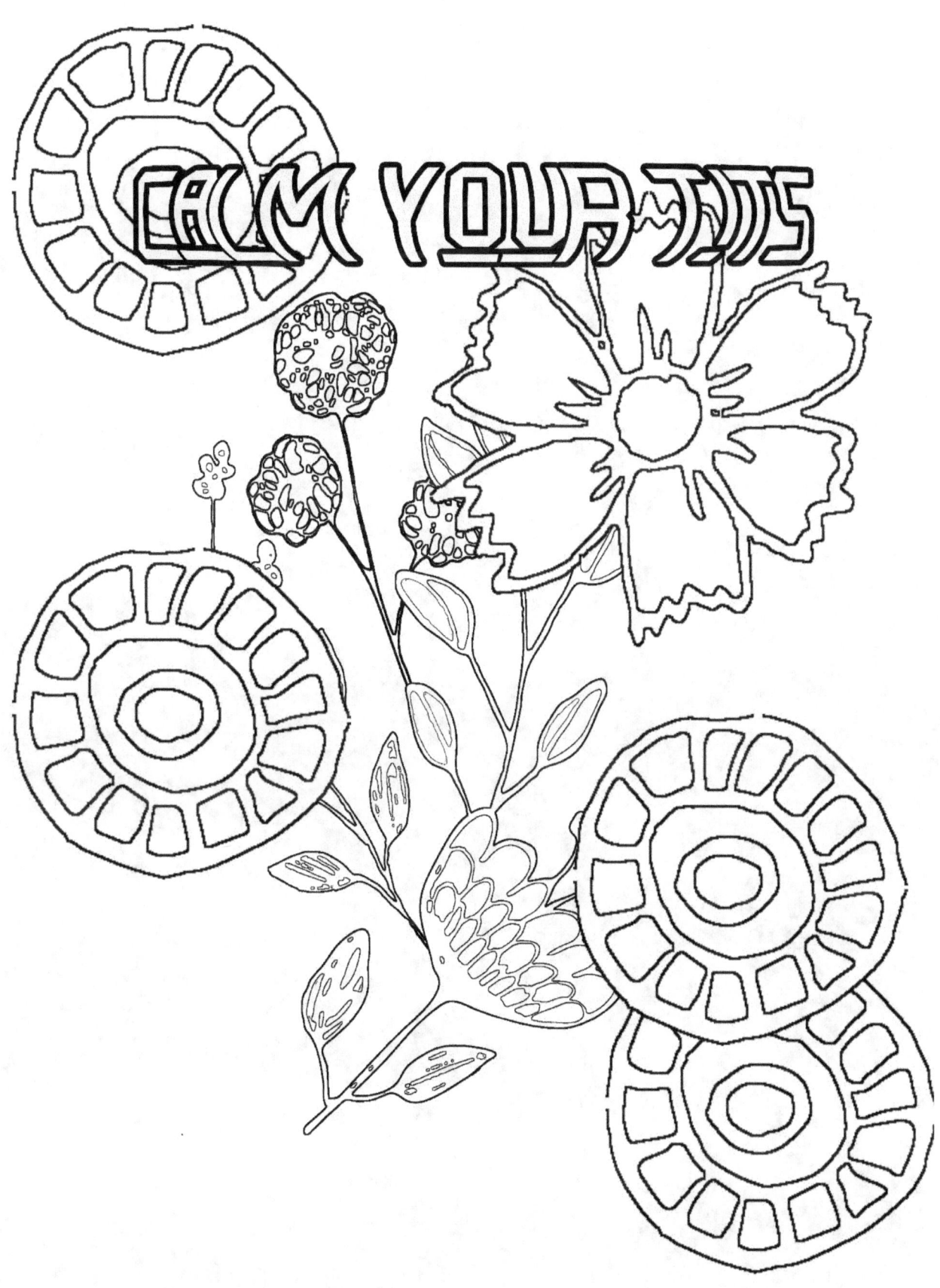

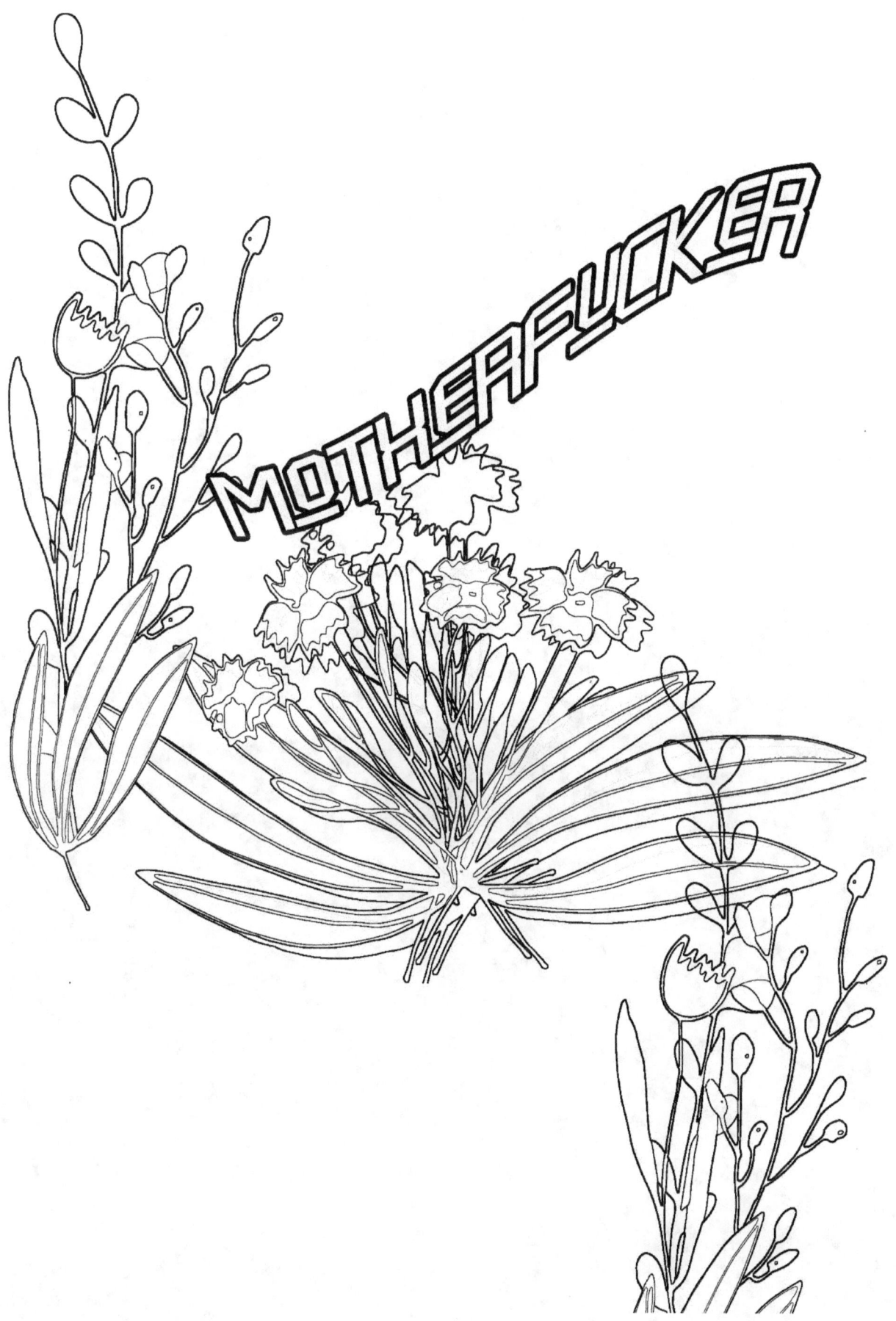

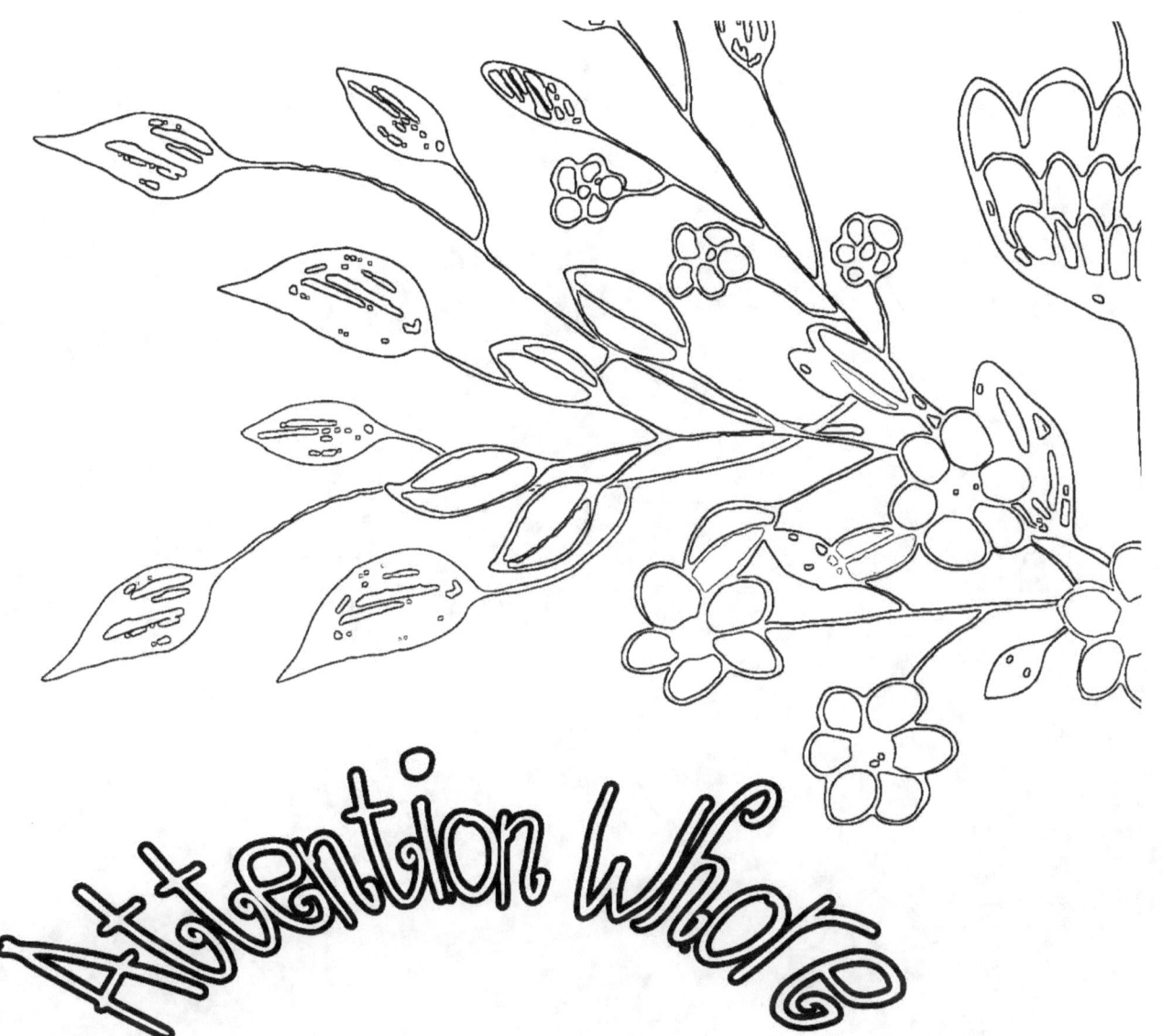

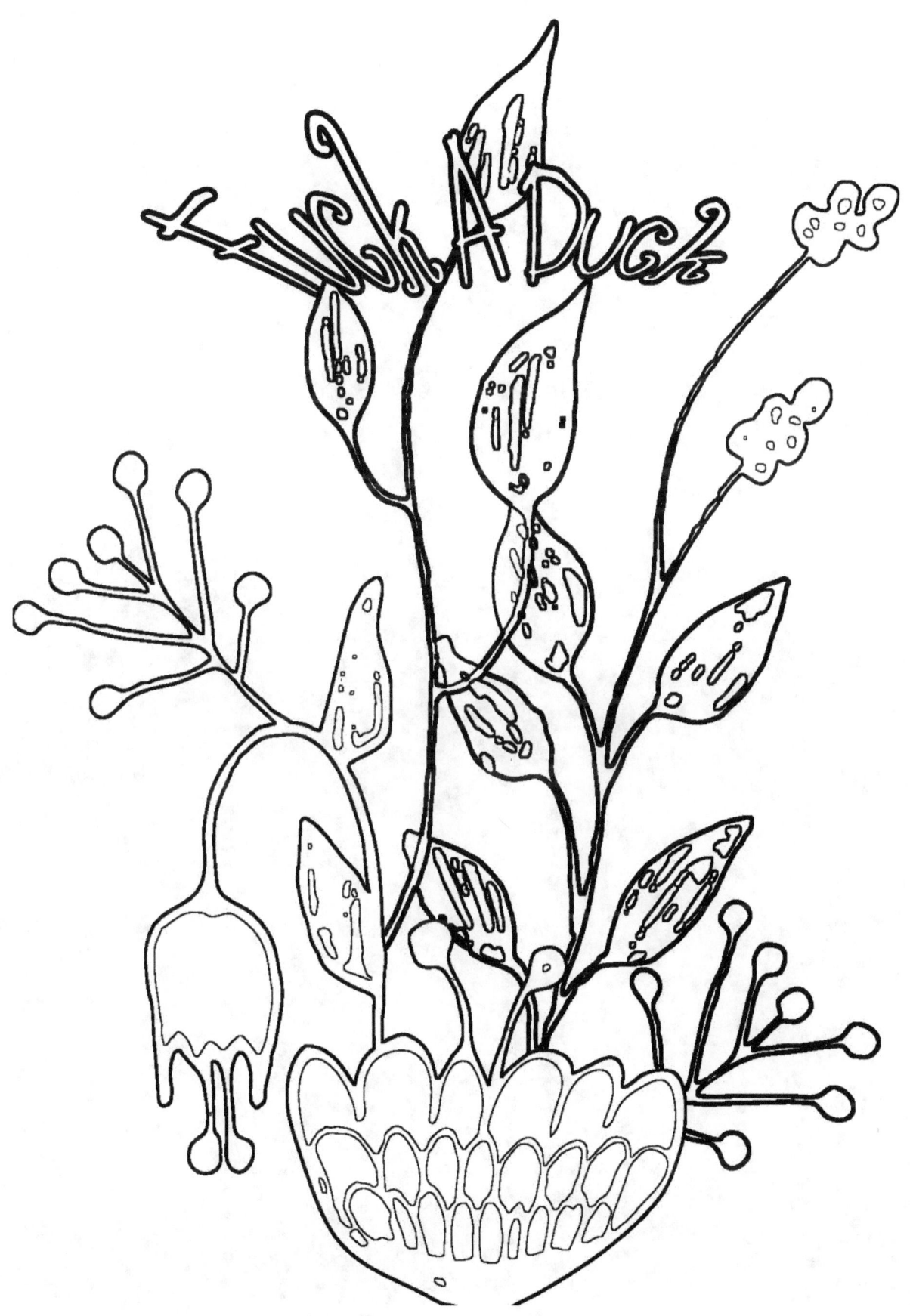

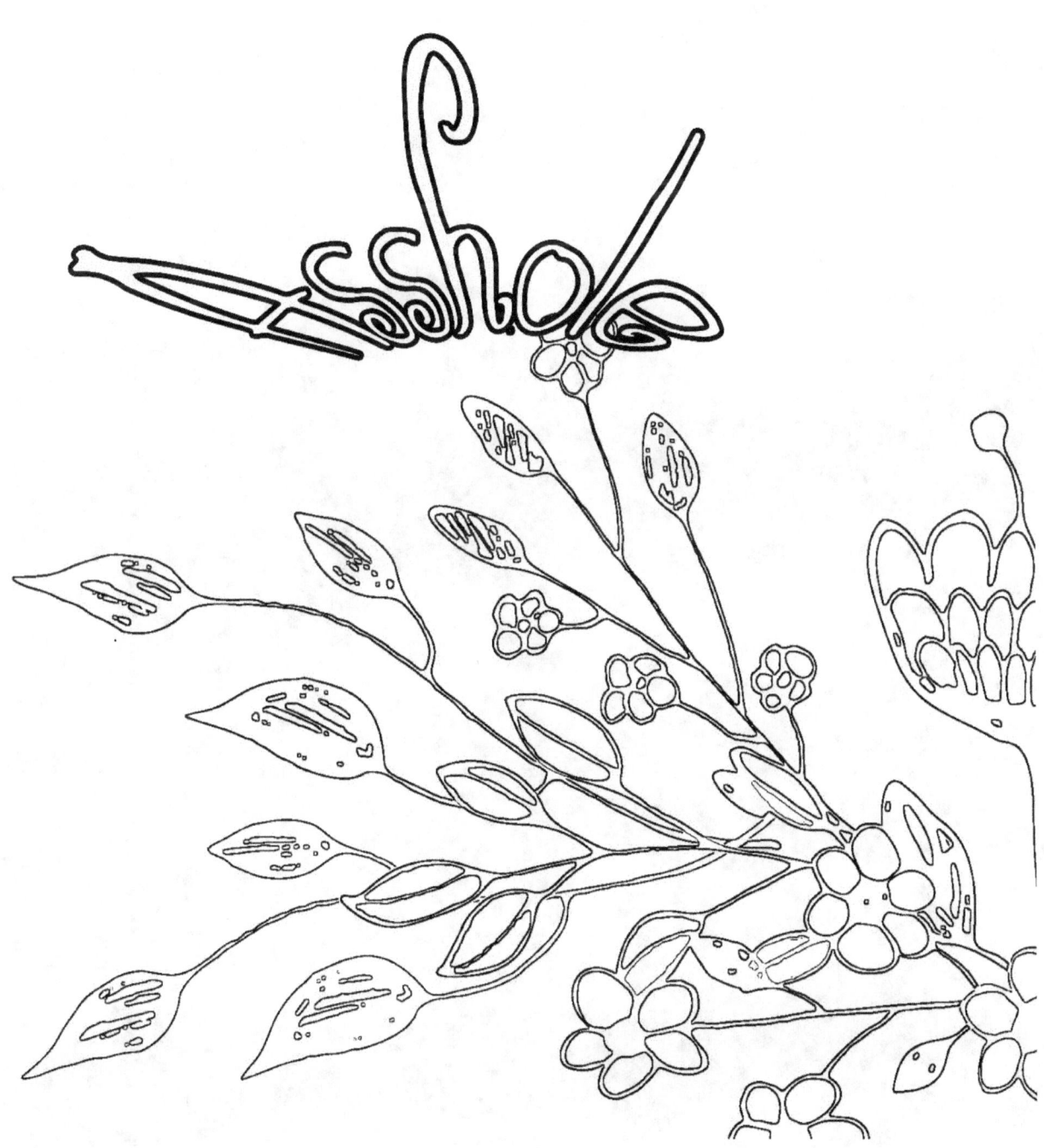

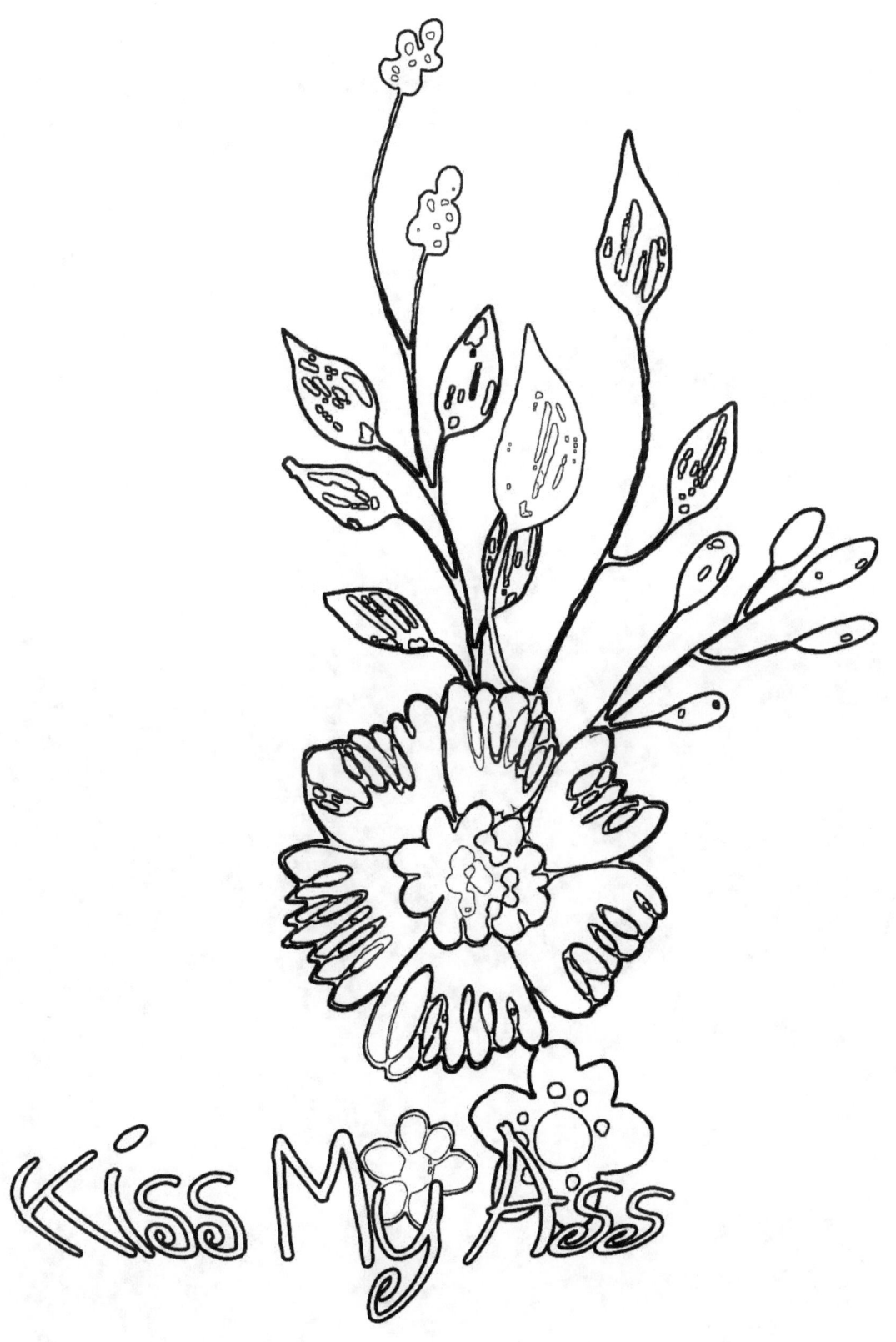

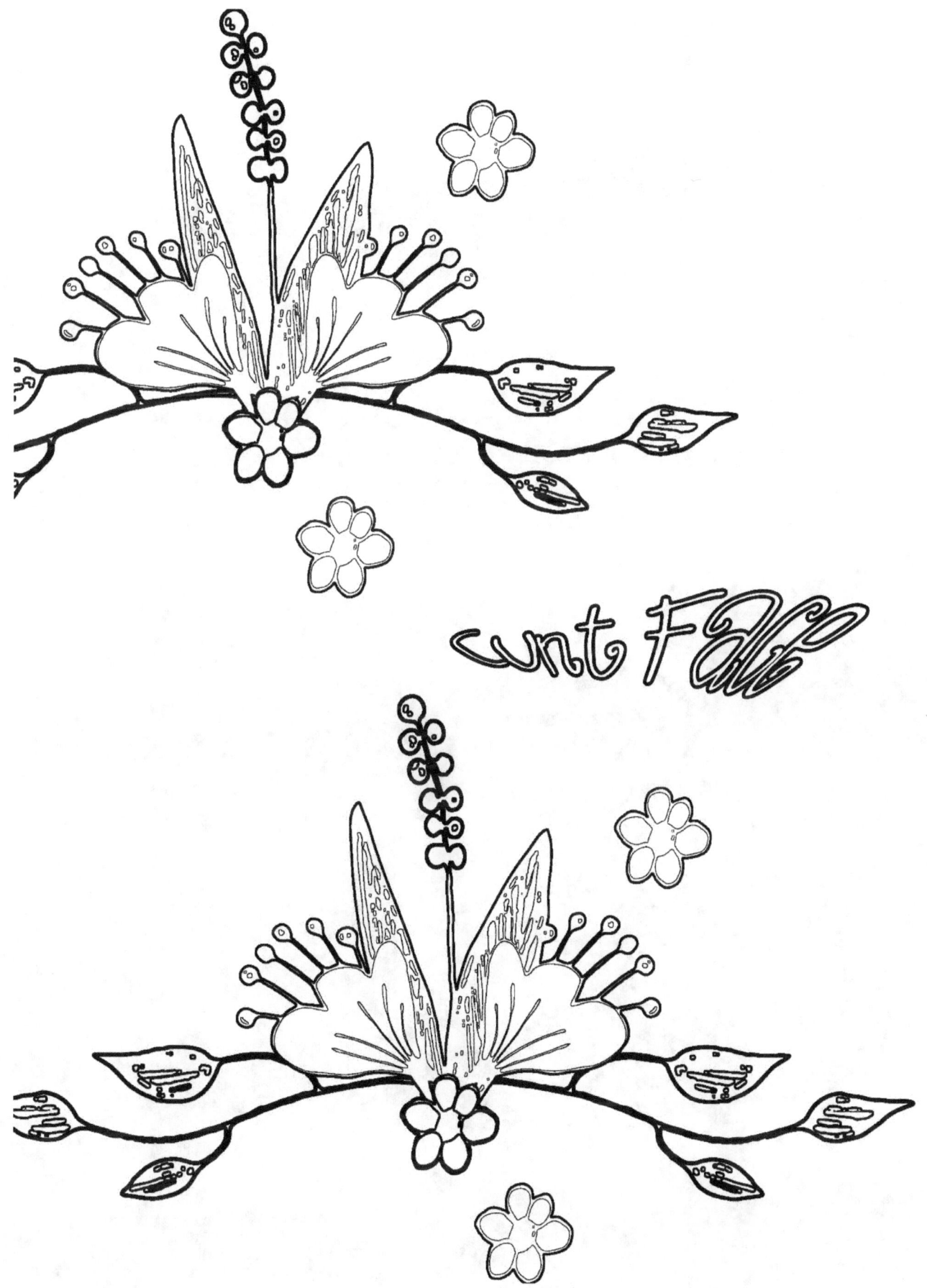

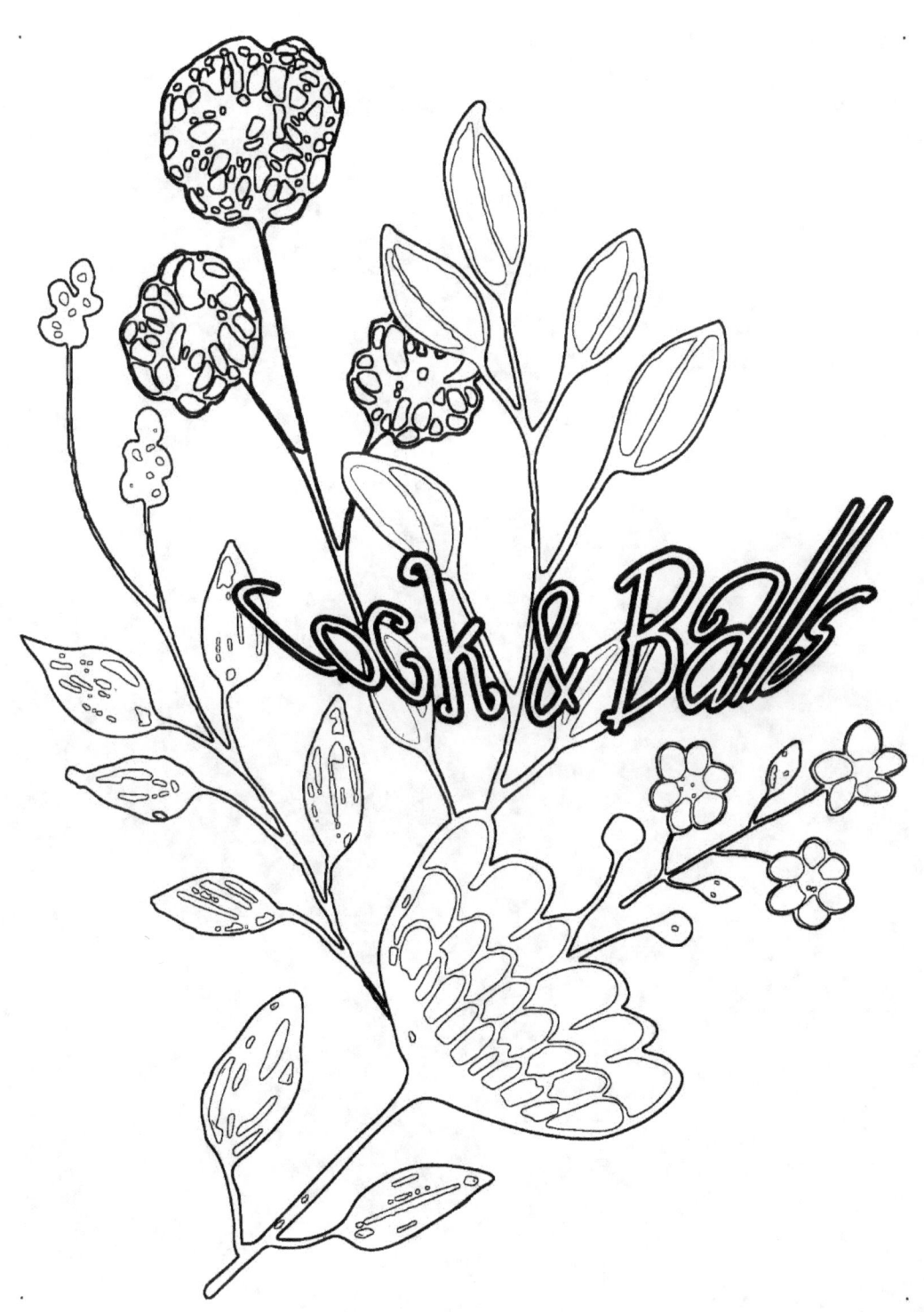

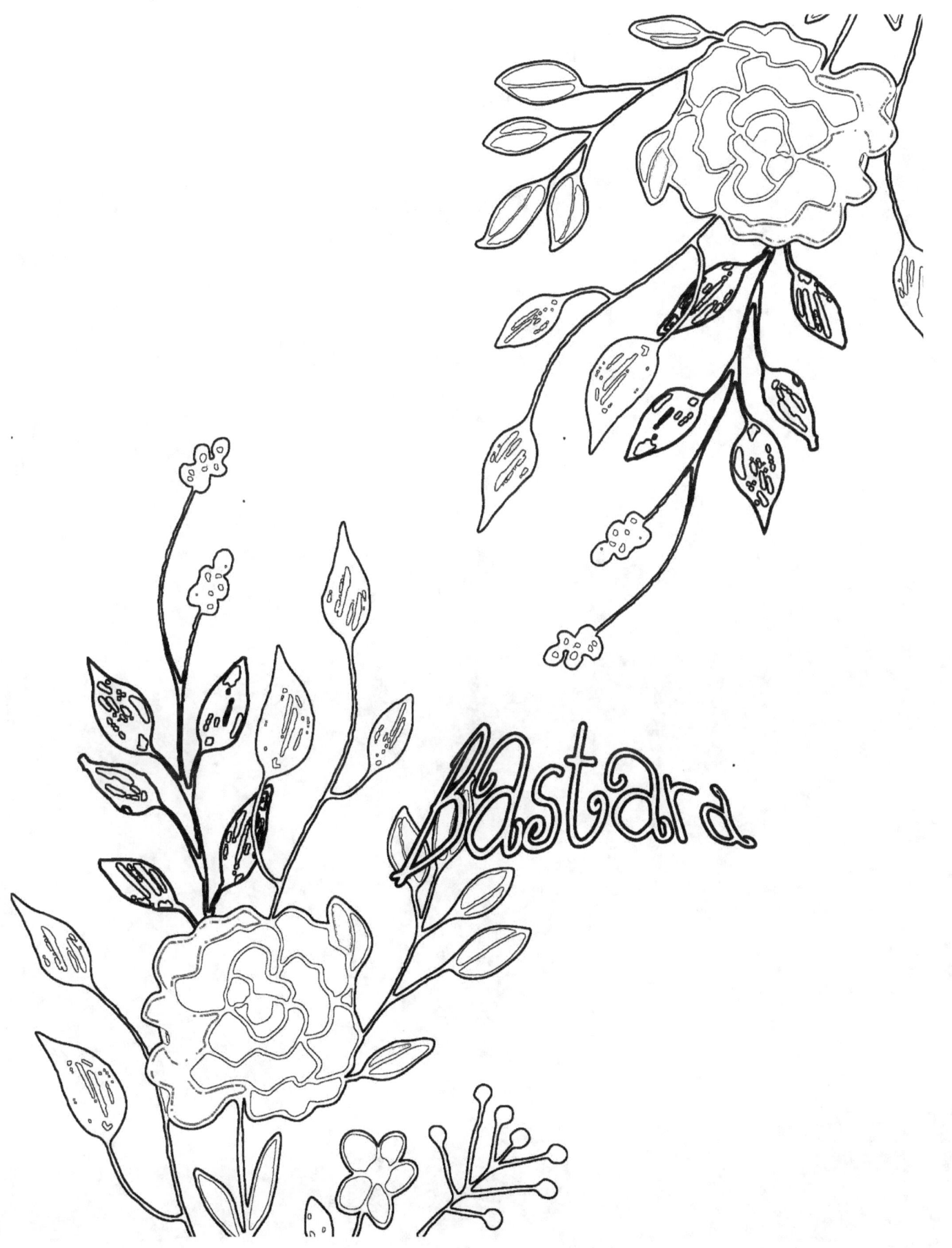

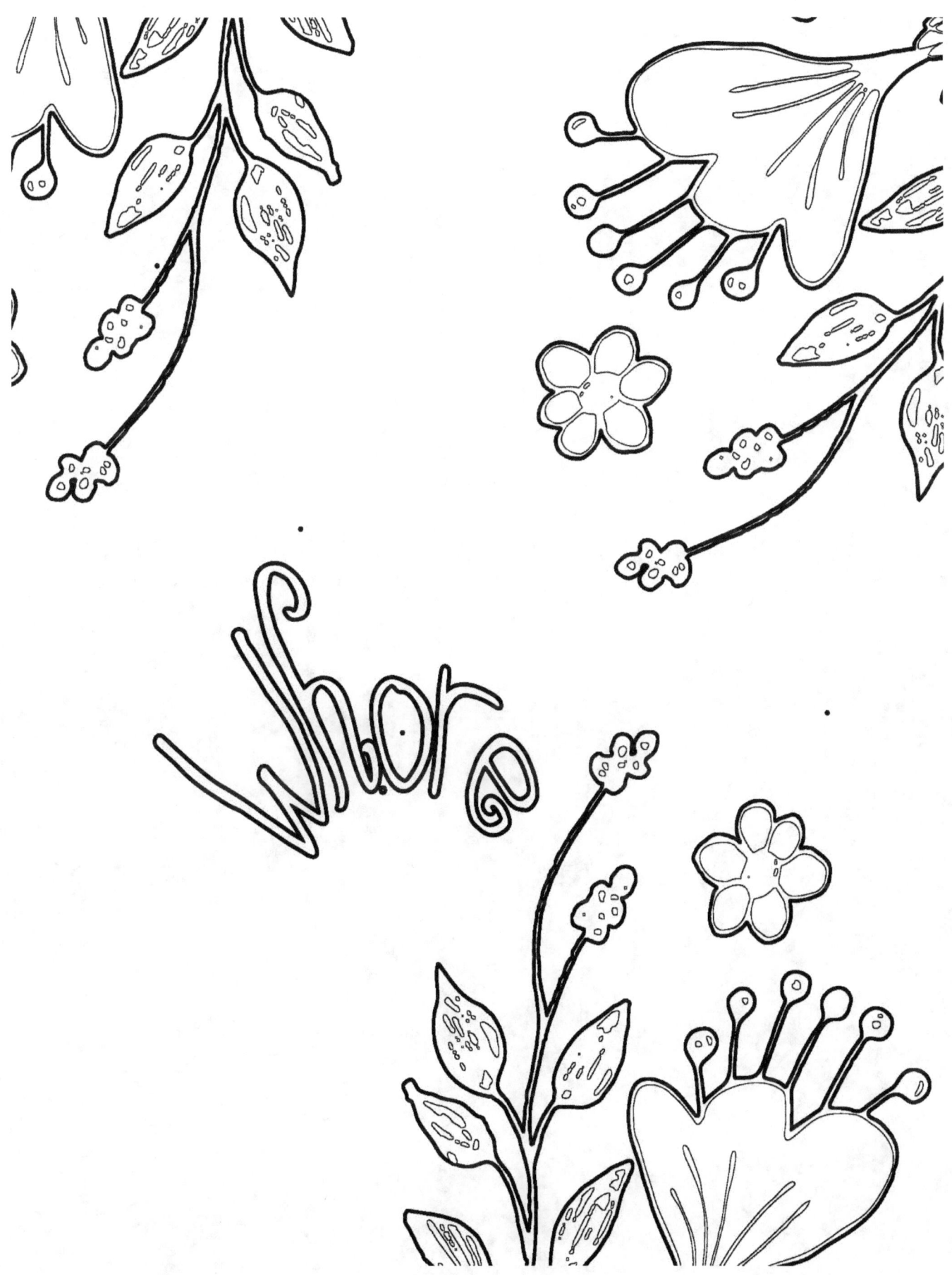

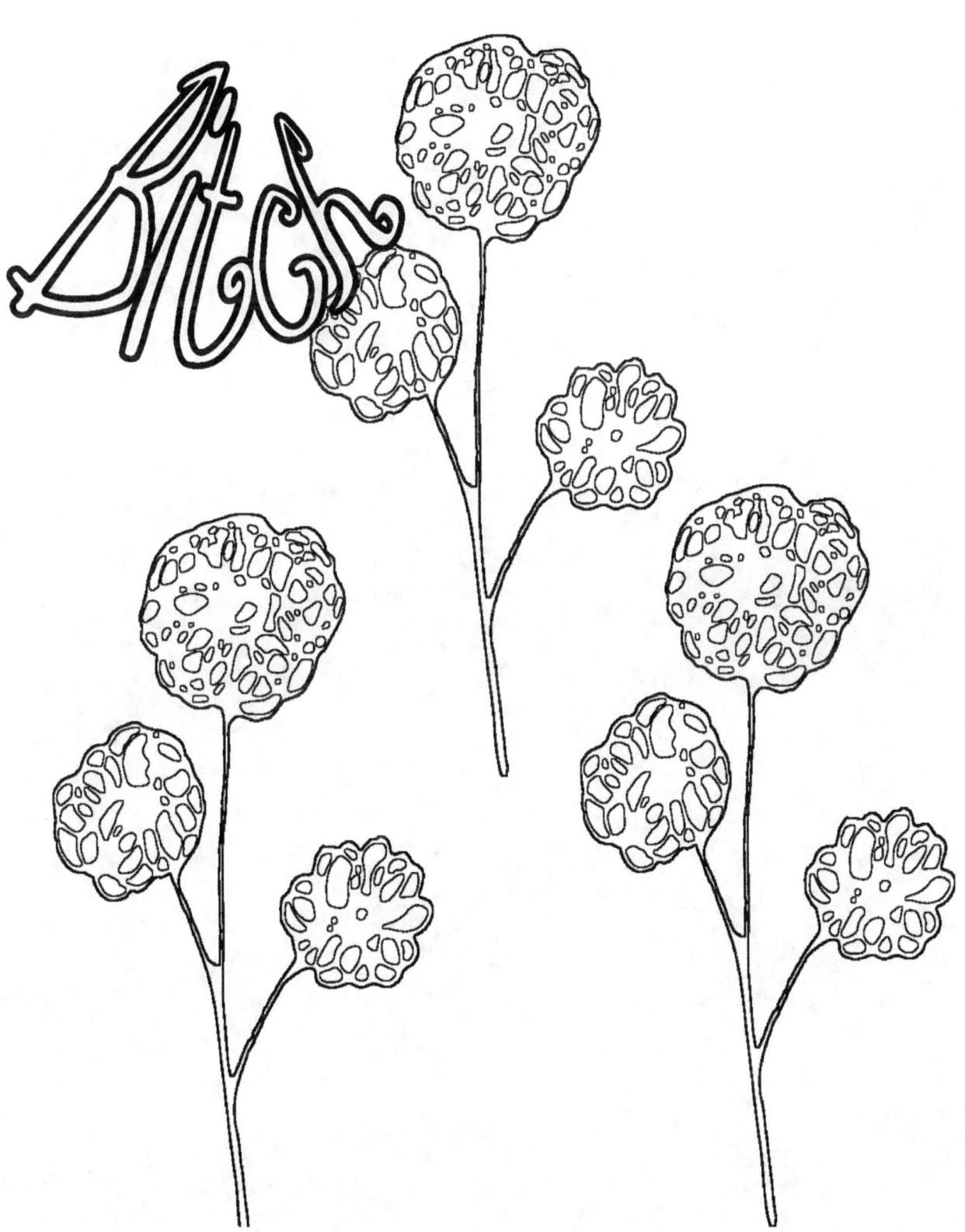

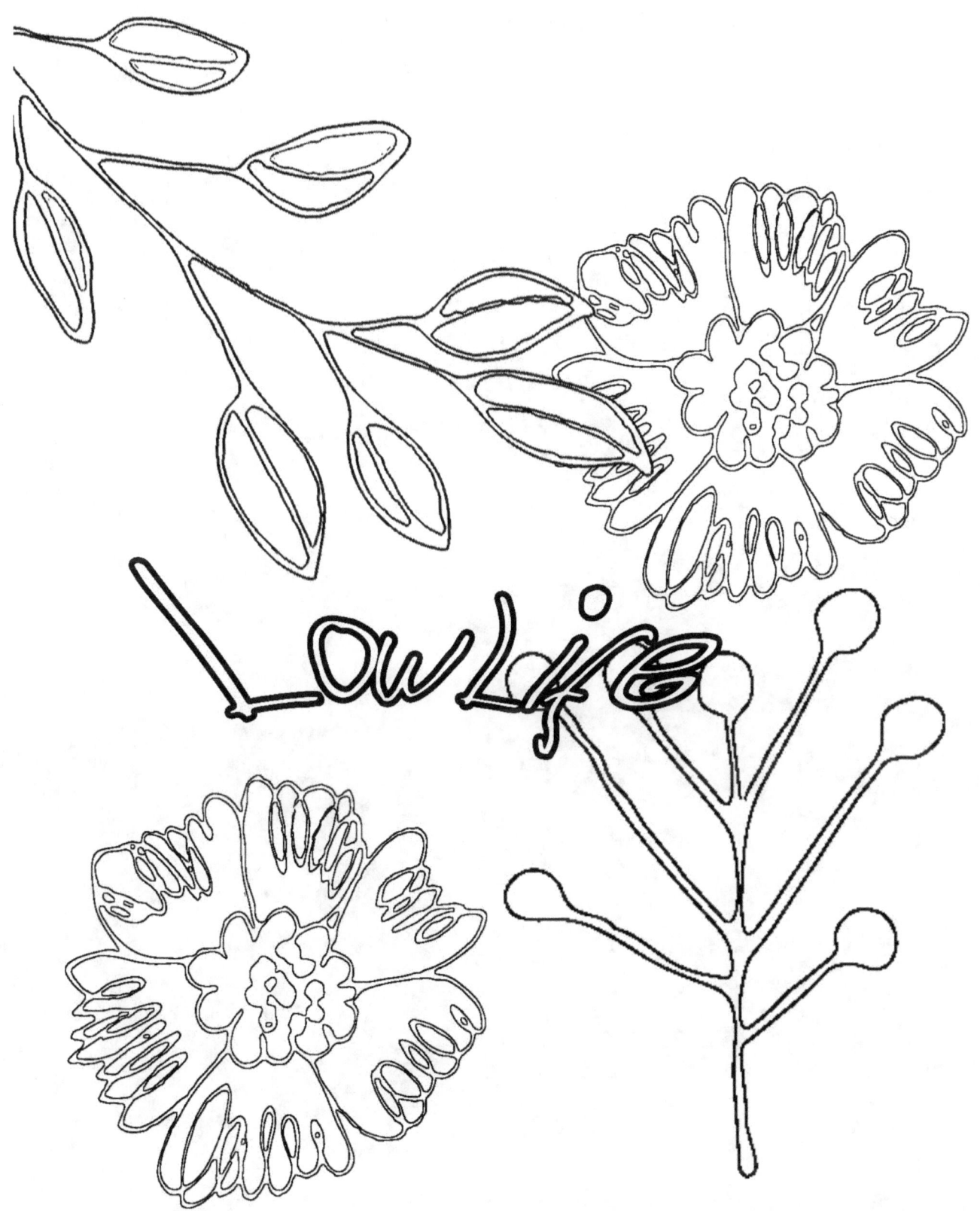

Holy Shit

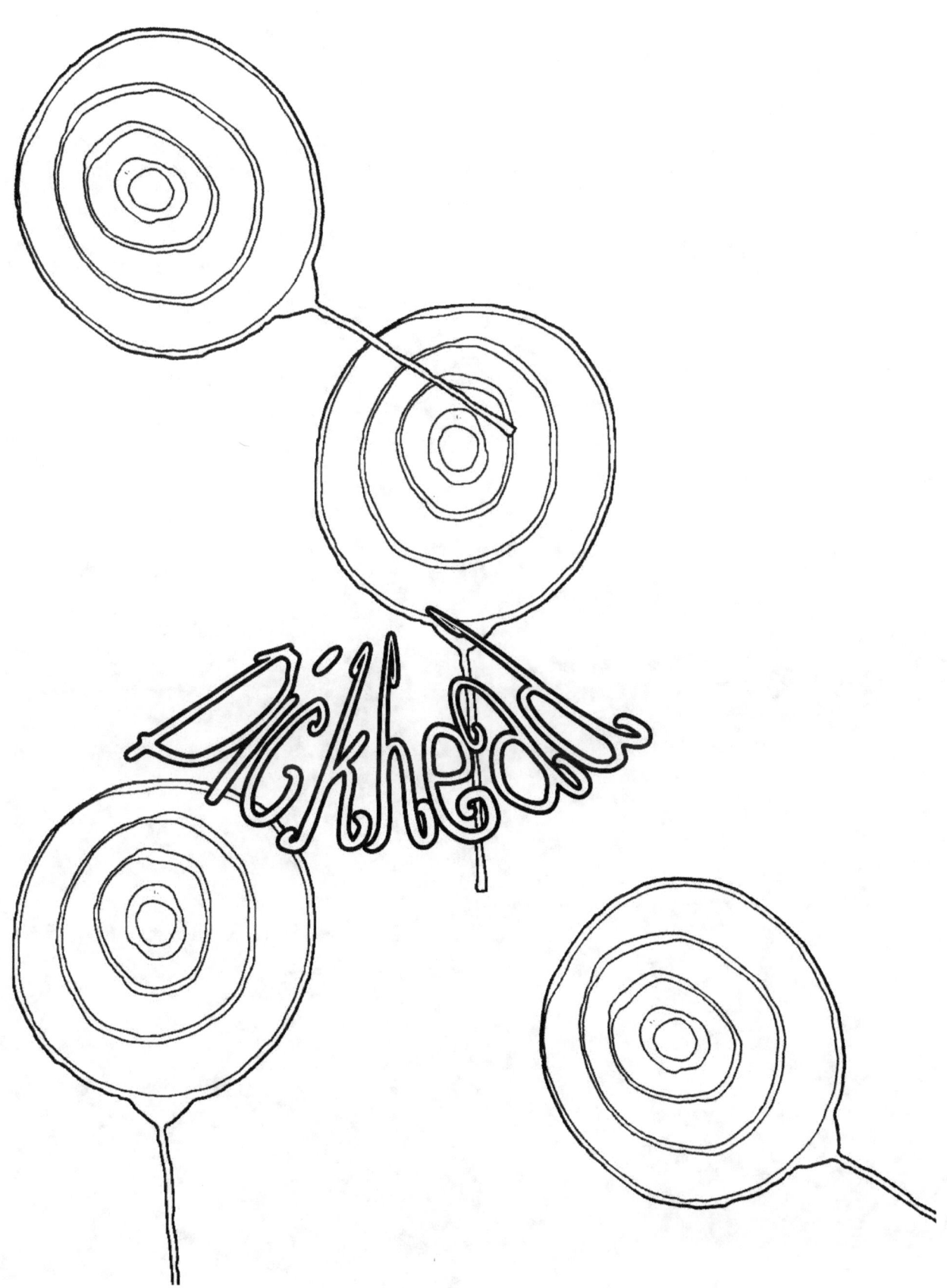

www.ingramcontent.com/pod-product-compliance
Lightning Source LLC
Chambersburg PA
CBHW081748170526
45167CB00009B/3965